W9-ATN-600

Prairie Dogs

by Caroline Arnold

illustrated by Jean Cassels

SCHOLASTIC INC.
New York Toronto London Auckland Sydney

It is early morning on the western prairie. To the east, the rising sun peeks over the horizon and warms the earth.

In their burrows underneath the ground, the prairie dogs are waking up. One by one they pop out of their holes. Soon you can see hundreds of prairie dogs!

They sniff the air. "Wee-o, wee-o," they call to each other.

A new day has begun in the prairie dog town.

Some prairie dog noises sound like barking. That's why we call them prairie dogs. But they are not dogs at all. They are really a kind of ground squirrel.

A prairie dog is about twice as big as a gray tree squirrel. An adult prairie dog weighs between two and four pounds. And from the tip of its nose to the tip of its tail, a prairie dog measures between 15 and 19 inches.

Squirrels belong to a group of animals called rodents. Rats, mice, and beavers are other kinds of rodents. Rodents have sharp front teeth. These teeth are always growing, so a rodent must gnaw to keep them worn down.

Prairie dogs use their teeth to eat prairie grass, seeds, roots, and other short plants. They also sometimes eat insects. Prairie dogs rarely drink. They get most of the water they need from the food they eat.

There are five species, or kinds, of prairie dogs: black-tailed, Mexican, white-tailed, Utah, and Gunnison's. The black-tailed and Mexican prairie dogs have black-tipped tails. They live in large groups called towns.

The slightly smaller white-tailed, Utah, and Gunnison's prairie dogs have white-tipped tails. They form smaller groups than their black-tailed relatives. Also, they make fewer sounds and spend less time together. They live at higher elevations on the western plains.

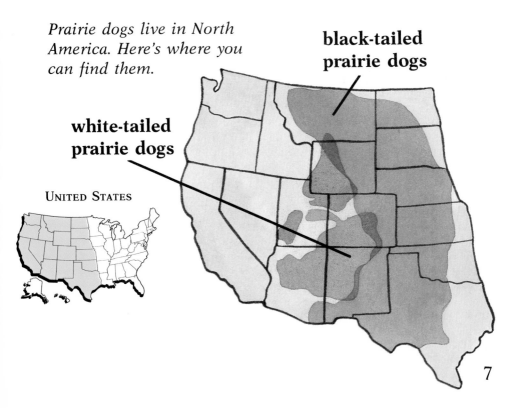

Prairie dogs live in North America. Here's where you can find them.

black-tailed prairie dogs

white-tailed prairie dogs

UNITED STATES

Once you could see prairie dog towns all over the West. Some were huge. One prairie dog town in Texas may have had 400 million prairie dogs in it!

Now most of those prairie dog towns are gone. Many farmers and ranchers think that prairie dogs are pests. They say that the prairie dogs eat too much grass. Also, cattle and horses sometimes step into the prairie dog holes and get hurt.

For many years people shot and poisoned prairie dogs. The Utah and Mexican prairie dogs are now in danger of becoming extinct.

Prairie dogs are the main food of black-footed ferrets. When people kill prairie dogs, the ferret has almost nothing to eat. Today, black-footed ferrets are nearly extinct, too.

Scientists watch prairie dogs to learn
more about them. They want to know:

Who lives in each prairie dog town?

Why do they behave the way they do?

Today a large black-tailed prairie dog
town may have hundreds of animals in it.
It may cover a square mile or more. Each
town includes several neighborhoods
called wards, and each ward is divided
into territories.

The group of prairie dogs that lives in a
territory is called a coterie (KO-ter-ee). Just
two prairie dogs or as many as several
dozen may belong to each coterie. A typical
group includes one adult male, several
adult females, and their youngsters. The
leader is the strongest male.

All the prairie dogs in a coterie know each other by their smell. When two prairie dogs meet, they touch noses. They also open their mouths and touch teeth. It looks as if they are kissing. They are really saying, "Hello. Who are you?"

Members of the same coterie are friendly to each other. After touching teeth, they may rub or lick each other. They may also use their paws to pick through each other's fur. This is called grooming. Grooming helps keep their fur clean and free of insects. It also helps the prairie dogs get to know each other better.

The territory of a coterie may be as small as a sandbox or as big as a football field. Members stand at the borders, point their noses to the sky, and yip. To other prairie dogs, this means, "This is where I live. Stay out!"

Most of the time, a prairie dog stays within the area of its own coterie. It eats, sleeps, and plays there. If it goes onto its neighbor's territory, the prairie dogs there will chase it back home.

The sloping sides of
the mound help keep
rain out of the burrow.

The longest burrows are more
than 100 feet. The shortest are
about 12 feet.

Prairie dogs have strong legs and sharp claws. They use them to dig burrows under the earth. At each burrow entrance, the prairie dogs pile dirt into a mound. Then they use their noses to press the dirt smooth.

Inside the burrow, the prairie dogs make long tunnels. These lead to rooms for sleeping, raising young prairie dogs, and storing food. The burrow also protects the prairie dogs from the weather. It stays cool in summer, and in winter it is warmer than the air outside.

The burrow may also have a room the prairie dogs use as a toilet.

Prairie dogs cut the plants around their burrows short. This helps the grass grow. It also makes predators easier to see.

A predator is an animal that hunts other animals for food. Here are some animals that hunt prairie dogs.

prairie falcon

red-tailed hawk

bobcat

badger

As soon as one prairie dog spots a predator, it gives the alarm call, "Chirk, chirk, chirk."

In a flash, all the prairie dogs dive to safety in their holes.

golden eagle

coyote

In the burrow there is a small ledge a few feet below the entrance. From there the prairie dogs can listen for the noises of animals above ground.

When all is quiet, one of the prairie dogs peeks out. If the danger is gone, the prairie dog jumps up and calls, "Wee-o, wee-o." Then the other prairie dogs know it is safe to go out.

Sometimes, prairie dogs need to repair their burrows because bison smash them. Bison often eat grass at the edge of a prairie dog town. They like to roll in the dirt of the prairie dog mounds. The dirt helps keep insects out of the bison's fur.

You might also see burrowing owls in a prairie dog town. They like to build their nests in old prairie dog holes.

Mating time for prairie dogs is in late winter and early spring. After mating, the female prairie dog is pregnant for four to five weeks.

Baby prairie dogs are called pups. A female prairie dog has one litter of pups a year. She may give birth to as many as ten pups. But usually she has about five.

While the female is waiting for her litter to be born, she collects dry grass. She puts it in her nesting room in the burrow. It will make a soft bed for the new pups.

At birth, each pup weighs about half an ounce, which is as much as a tablespoon of peanut butter. It cannot see or hear and it has no fur.

The tiny prairie dogs snuggle close to their mother. They drink milk from the teats on her belly. They will drink milk until they are seven weeks old.

Young prairie dogs grow quickly. Soon they can hear, and their fur begins to grow. Their eyes open when they are almost five weeks old.

Inside the burrow, young prairie dogs sometimes wander into another nest. The female there will allow them to drink milk along with her own pups.

Recently, scientists noticed a strange thing. Sometimes a prairie dog mother kills the newborn pups of another female in her coterie. Scientists do not know why she does this. Perhaps she is hungry. Perhaps it keeps the coterie from becoming too crowded. Scientists are still looking for answers to this question.

When prairie dog pups are about five weeks old, they come out of the burrow for the first time.

They begin to eat grass and find their own food. They learn to watch for danger. They pester the adults for grooming. And they chase each other and tumble on the ground.

At first the adult prairie dogs allow youngsters from nearby coteries to visit. Later, when the young prairie dogs grow bigger, they are chased home.

A prairie dog reaches its adult size when it is about six months old. Female prairie dogs stay in the same coterie for their whole lives. They live to be about seven years old.

In its second year, a young male leaves the coterie where it was born. It fights to become a leader in another coterie. Or it may start a new coterie. Males usually live to be about five years old.

As summer comes to an end, the days grow short and cool. The prairie dogs eat and eat. Their bodies grow plump. The fat helps keep them warm. It also provides energy.

A black-tailed prairie dog is active in winter. But food is hard to find. On stormy days, the prairie dog stays underground. It lives on its fat and eats food stored in the burrow.

A white-tailed prairie dog hibernates (HY-bur-nates) in winter. It curls up in its burrow and goes to sleep. Its body temperature drops. It does not wake up until spring. Then it is time to start a new prairie dog year.

Index

About the Author

Caroline Arnold is the author of more than eighty books for children, including award-winning titles such as *Koala*, *Saving the Peregrine Falcon*, and *Dinosaur Mountain*. When she was growing up in Minneapolis, Minnesota, she spent her summers at a camp in northern Wisconsin. That is where she first developed her interest in animals and the out-of-doors.

Today she goes to zoos, museums, and wild-life parks as part of the research for her books. For this book she visited prairie dog towns in Utah and Arizona. Ms. Arnold lives in Los Angeles, California, with her husband, who is a neuroscientist, and their two children. Ms. Arnold also teaches part-time in the Writers' Program at UCLA Extension.

If You Want to Read More About Prairie Dogs:

The Friendly Prairie Dog, by Denise Casey (Dodd, Mead and Company, 1987).

Come Visit a Prairie Dog Town, by Eugenia Alston (Harcourt Brace Jovanovich, 1976).

"Prairie Dog," *Book of Mammals, Vol. 2* (National Geographic Society, 1981).

Library of Congress Cataloging-in-Publication Data

Arnold, Caroline.
Prairie dogs / by Caroline Arnold; illustrations by Jean Cassels.
p.   cm.
Includes bibliographical references and index.
Summary: Describes a year in the life of prairie dogs during which
they build and repair tunnels, find food, rear young, elude predators,
and prepare for winter.
ISBN 0-590-46946-0
1. Prairie dogs — Juvenile literature. [1. Prairie dogs.]
I. Cassels, Jean, ill. II. Title.
QL737.R68A76   1993
599.32′32 — dc20   92-38283
                                                          CIP
                                                          AC

12 11 10 9 8 7 6 5 4 3 2 1   3 4 5 6 7 8/9

Printed in the U.S.A.   23

First Scholastic printing, September 1993

Book design by Laurie McBarnette.